Overcoming Depression and Anxiety for the Average Joe

Overcoming Depression and Anxiety for the Average Joe

Jeff Fredericks

Library of Congress Control Number:		2010904572
ISBN:	Hardcover	978-1-4500-7099-7
	Softcover	978-1-4500-7098-0
	Ebook	978-1-4500-7100-0

To order additional copies of this book, contact:
Xlibris Corporation
1-888-795-4274
www.Xlibris.com
Orders@Xlibris.com
79051

Dedication

This book is dedicated to those suffering from anxiety and depression and those that have lost their lives due to it. It is also dedicated to the survivors of those who lost loved ones. It also is dedicated to Mary, who without her guidance and understanding, I may not be writing this today.

Foreword

Namaste. Many years ago I found myself suffering from deep depression and horrible anxiety. I suffered a breakdown and had to be hospitalized. I recall asking God, "Why is this happening to me?" The answer I heard deep inside me was, "When you recover, go and help others."

This book is my feeble attempt to do just that. I am no expert. I do not have a degree in the subject matter. I do not pretend to have all the answers.

I only have my answers. These I will share with you for whatever they are worth. I will give you my highlight reel as it were to show how I ended up there, from my humble beginnings, to my arrival at that dark time in my life, to the recovery, and to the now.

I have been free with no relapses for almost twenty-five years.

I must therefore be doing something that at least works for myself.

Perhaps my methods will help others. Maybe at least get them to think to find even a better way. I give full credit to a higher power, God, or the universe, whatever is deemed appropriate to you. I did not survive this of my own accord. I was indeed helped. I share with you in these pages that follow my story.

1

It was a warm evening that July of nineteen eighty seven. The major league all star game was to be played. This would be the first one I would not see on television since I fell in love with baseball back when I was ten years old.

I had not been feeling well. I had no idea what was wrong. I had been getting dizzy at work, feeling like I was going to pass out. I felt drained, as if I had no strength at all. Also, I was having trouble getting to sleep, if at all. For lack of a better description, I felt like I would implode.

I had been to the doctor. He had put me on an anti-depressant and told me to check back if I did not feel better. At this point the anxiety attacks as I would later learn what they were, had finally caught up with me.

I was living alone at the time, so I called my parents. "Please help me, I do not know what's wrong," I recall saying. They knew what I had been going through. My mother asked if I wanted to go to the crisis center at the hospital. I finally surrendered and said "yes."

I had gone deep within myself to the point of not being able to get out. I had never felt this afraid in my life. I recall suffering from viral encephalitis years ago. The headache from that was so severe I had actually considered taking my life. Fortunately, I recovered from it. This type of pain was different. It was worse.

After being evaluated I was diagnosed as suffering from depression and anxiety. I would be admitted and kept for weeks as the medication built up in my system.

How did I get to this point? To make that clear, I will go back to the beginning.

"Wow it's dark in here!" Okay, I am joking, I'm not going that far back!

I was the oldest of six children. The guinea pig or the crash test dummy as it were. I would actually become the latter in time as I became older. But I will get to that in time. My parents had a pattern down, boy, girl, boy, girl, boy, girl. Every time Dad received a raise, Mom became pregnant! If you didn't laugh, please reread that line and come back! Actually it was pretty close to the truth.

As far as I could recall at the time I was hospitalized, my memories of a childhood were fairly normal. At least up until age nine. Perhaps eight. Somewhere in that time period.

I recall moving a few times early on. At age five we moved from Sayre, Pennsylvania to Endwell, New York. I would be starting school. Sayre left me with some good memories and some good friends, but I adapted easily and made new ones in my new surroundings. I started kindergarten in a public school, rode the school bus and seemed to enjoy it. First grade was within walking distance. It was a catholic school.

My first day at catholic school was interesting. I recall coming home and informing my mother that the men there were very nice, but I just did not understand their uniforms. Mom told me that they were Nuns and were women. I of course refused this diagnosis and argued with my mother that they were indeed men. I eventually bought it, but it took a bit of convincing. After all why would women wear such ugly shoes? Not to mention the rest of the ridiculous outfits and head gear?!

Anyway grades one through four then were great. I enjoyed the way I was treated by my peers, I liked to learn, and I did great with my grades. However sometime after I reached the age of reason, most experts say around seven years of age, I began to experience some very unpleasant things at home.

As I developed my personality and began being who I was at the time, my Dad began to beat me. This really sucked. I was my father's son. He was my hero. I looked up to him. It was terrorizing to me in more than one way. It was horrible enough getting beat up and verbally abused, but by the man I loved and cherished, it was devastating.

It was not every day but any time I was in trouble or did something wrong that it happened. What was worse was that it only happened to me. My father was verbally abusive to all of us, but I alone was the physically abused.

Dad was an ex-Navy man that did his term and went to work for a large blue chip company that I would later also have a career with. He married my mother shortly thereafter and was working eight to ten hour days. He would eventually discover that a high school degree and service time would not bring home the money or prestige he craved. Therefore, he started commuting an hour away to college at night after work to earn his degree.

I can now as an adult appreciate the hours and stress he went through for us. The beatings I never did. I eventually would come to however. Weekends were tough as well because Dad would coop himself up in a room to study. Time with him was at a premium. My highlight reel was often having my ass kicked.

Let me set the record straight though. My Dad is and was also a very funny and supportive man who I loved, and love dearly. There were and still are great times with him. The Jekyll/Hyde years were crazy however.

The other part of those early years were surrounding my mother. She had suffered a breakdown while Dad was doing his thing with corporate America and school. My mother had just lost her father to early death, her grandmother whom she revered, and a cousin near her age or very close to it. Those deaths, coupled with her hero John F. Kennedy being assassinated and having four children in a row, overwhelmed her.

Mom was obviously fried. Between the afore mentioned, and caring for all these children with no other adults around, she had a breakdown. She was twenty seven years old at the time. I also had my breakdown at the same age.

Things were tough during the time Mom was hospitalized. The beatings were more frequent. But at least I had catholic school and its attitudes and disciplines to keep me sane. I also had my brothers and sisters and friends.

Mom eventually recovered after shock treatment and came home. She was different and more distant, but she was home. After my youngest brother was born, my father decided we needed a bigger house. He had one built in Apalachin, New York. New house, new neighborhood, new school. Things were about to get ugly.

Apalachin at the time, at least the area of it we moved to, was somewhere between rural and suburbia. Our development was all new, but the surrounding area was older and more spaced out. It felt like we were "out in the sticks."

The local kids were a much different breed than I had encountered before. Once school started I found out just how different.

I had begun to cower like a dog that had been beat too much. I always stood up for myself early on. Once the beatings started, I eventually just surrendered and covered. It seems the local kids and the ones at school noticed this.

Back in catholic school, we had no gymnasium. Therefore I never learned any type of sports at all. My father was not an outdoorsman, and he was not free or around the house that much. As soon as the kids in school saw that I had no athletic abilities, or knowledge of any sports, I was doomed.

I also had been used to dressing for school in a uniform. Now I could dress as I wished. We had good income so I dressed slightly left of center as it were. At the time my features were somewhat more on the feminine side as well. I became a very easy target of ridicule. Children can be mean and they were. I was now getting picked on and beat up at school, at play in my neighborhood, and at home by my father.

Gym class was especially terrorizing. It was bad enough being picked last for team sports, picked on in general, but then . . . . we had to take showers! "Oh my God!" I had to let people see me naked?! I wanted no part of this. My teacher finally made me take one. The kids of course saw I was nervous and jumped all over me teasing. The next four years were very much like this. A few bright spots opened up. I did find a few friends but they picked on me as well. But they liked me and did not harm me. I also fell in love with baseball. I wanted to spend more time with Dad. We finally signed up for cable television which we never had before. I recall coming down to the family room to find Dad watching an exhibition baseball game in mid March.

"I never knew you liked baseball?" I said. "Who is playing?" He told me it was the New York Mets and some one else I do not recall. He began explaining the game to me. It turned out to be an enjoyable evening. I later learned more about the game from a neighbor friend who also helped me play and join little league.

It was awesome to find something else I really sucked at! I was now the laughingstock of the league. I was really consistent! But I did love this game, and I did love my Mets. This of course did not bode well either as the Mets had only been around seven years and always finished last. That and the fact that this was Yankee country just gave everyone else more ammunition to fire at me.

I somehow managed to survive those years and slowly began to fit in. My grades were suffering though. It was hard to concentrate, and motivation was lacking. I would now get beat up and over punished for bad report cards.

I eventually learned to hide them and not bring them home. Of course the cat would find its way out of the bag and my parents would find out. I would get it anyway. Deferred with interest.

During this time I met a friend that was genuine. His name was Rudy. He liked me just the way I was. I really loved him. We were getting along and just starting to become close friends. This was a very brief period however. I remember being on Easter recess. The evening prior, I had been bicycling with Rudy. We had been down by the creek and riding the trails and back to the school yard. We had been talking about the things friends talked about. He would be busy with his family for the next few days, and then we could play again together after that. I could not wait to see him again.

Mom had called me in the house early the next evening prior to dinner. She asked me to sit down. I knew I was in trouble for something, just not sure what. What came next was unexpected and hurt more than any beating I had received.

"Rudy died today." Mom said. "What do you mean he died?!!" I asked shocked. She explained that there had been an accident. Rudy was riding a raft in the creek with his cousins. The raft capsized and everyone went into the water. Rudy tried to save his cousin as he was a good swimmer, and she could not swim. They both drowned while he tried to save her. I was stunned.

I recall going to the funeral and the wake. I had so many feelings going on that I could not separate or identify them.

I had never seen either of my parents cry. While getting teased at school and everywhere else I found it also a good idea not to allow anyone seeing me cry. So when Rudy died, I did not cry even though I was hurting inside. This was to become very detrimental in the future. "Men do not cry". I had heard it from many sources and it was learned by example in my home.

Now that I was sure God hated me, I decided to become an altar boy at church. No one bothered me at church, and perhaps God would take pity on me and ease up a bit.

These times were actually good times. I bonded with other alter boys and with the priests and ushers. It was almost like catholic school again. At least in the part that it was, or felt safe to me.

During this time I actually thought about becoming a priest. It was a step up from my younger years of wanting to be a garbage man! Yes, I had a garbage truck fetish in Endwell. Those trucks fascinated me! Anyway, the problem with being a priest was not being able to marry.

I had always wanted to get married from a very young age. At this point in time, I did not know why. But I did. That being said, being an altar boy was an interest of only a few years. By fourteen I had outgrown it. I had not much luck with girls yet. Most were brief crushes where the girl I liked could not stand me, or the girl that liked me, I could not stand!

At thirteen and a half however after finding someone I liked and liked me back, nothing happened! I liked this girl Kelly and later found out she actually liked me. I was so mesmerized that someone I liked also liked me that I did nothing about it! I did not know how. So Kelly moved on and I was left to my self pity and loss.

A few months later Cynthia came along, with an interest in me. She was cute and not bad at all for being a year older. She was probably not someone I would have sought out on my own, but after losing and not entering into a relationship with Kelly, I was not going to let Cynthia get away.

I recall the fireworks and elation of experiencing our, or at least my first kiss. I had no clue what I was doing, but I really liked it! We did the things that young people do in their first relationship at that age. We talked on the phone, went to school dances, held hands in school while walking in the hall. It felt good to be wanted. It felt good to fit in.

The guys that picked on me still liked to call me an asshole while she was with me, but we ignored them. I enjoyed the high of being accepted and wanted.

Cynthia and I went our separate ways after six months. I ended it. It was nothing personal, I just wanted to try on a relationship, and I did like her. At best it was puppy love, if that. I wanted to date other girls and I also knew that I was not in love. I was almost fourteen and unknowingly entering a very important time in my life. Things were about to change dramatically. Change for the better, but not before getting worse.

My Dad being an only child had one very close friend who he considered a brother. It was the only family to him other than his parents.

Louie was a priest. He had been instrumental in my parents meeting. He also had an influence on them getting married. I always considered him an uncle. He was a loving, caring man. He was a tough guy as well. He signed up for the Viet Nam war and went in not only as a chaplain, but as a Green Beret!

We were proud of him, yet always concerned because of his surroundings. We had lost our neighborhood paper carrier in Endwell to that war. My Uncle Bert had also been there as well, but returned safely. Louie also returned home after his tour. He then became a member of the National Guard.

In June of the year of my fourteenth birthday, Hurricane Agnes came up the coast and flooded the Wilkes-Barre, Pennsylvania area where my parents and grandparents were from. Fortunately my grandparents did not get hit from the floodwaters. But when the waters receded we went down to visit.

While we were touring the area, a National Guard jeep pulled us over as they were assigned to the crisis there. My Dad pulled over thinking he had done something wrong or was driving in an area he should not be.

The tall army guy came up to the driver's window and said or rather asked, "you going somewhere mister?" It was Louie! We were thrilled to see him, especially my Dad. We had a mini re-union right there. Louie told stories of riding his bicycle from town to town to say Mass for the soldiers while bombs exploded around him in Viet Nam. He was glad to be home.

After our visit there we returned home. It was mid summer of nineteen seventy-two. I was almost fourteen and had flourished into a six foot tall frame.

I do not recall what I did or what angered my father, but he came after me with his fists. I grabbed him by the neck and chest and crashed him into the wall near the bottom of the stairs. "It ends now!" I commanded. I recall how surprised and white he became. "You will never touch me again, understand?!" He said nothing as I released him and backed away. I was angry enough to kill him, but he was my Dad. The good thing was after that day, there was never again a hand laid on me. We still had arguments and went nose to nose occasionally, but the home beatings were now a thing of the past.

A few days before my birthday, my mother came into my bedroom very early asking me to turn on my six-band radio which was capable of picking up radio stations from the area my grandparents were from.

"What's wrong?" I asked. Mom said "Get the Wilkes-Barre station news, your Aunt just called and thought she heard that Louie was killed in a car accident!" I froze momentarily, and then did as requested. It was only a short while before confirmation occurred. Louie, we would later learn, rented a cabin with a gang of childhood friends near his home parish. They took turns mowing the lawn. Louie was finishing when his friends were leaving. They had asked him to leave with them, to leave the last patch of lawn, but he insisted on finishing it.

It was dark by the time he must have left. He jumped on his motorcycle and began riding down the hill on the main road. A jeep came around the bend and plowed into Louie. The driver was drunk.

Dad was away in Dallas, Texas when Mom called him through tears to report the awful news. I recall later Dad telling me that when Mom told him, he swung around in shock and anger to be staring at the school book depository from which Lee Harvey Oswald had worked.

A few days later we were at the funeral home for the wake. In Pennsylvania the coffins were full lid open, not split lid like New York. This is important to mention for this reason . . . Louie was positioned in the coffin head where the feet go and feet where the head usually goes. Why? He was basically pieced together by the mortician. From what I was later told, he was blasted in pieces all over the road. He was turned in the coffin to show the better side. He was also buried in white rather than the traditional purple because his pastor believed him to be a saint.

Dad went up to pay his respects. After doing this, he went to reach out into the coffin to touch Louie. Louie's sister jumped up to stop my father from doing so. "John," she said to my father, "We can not touch him or he may fall apart." I will never forget this moment as long as I live. Louie was indeed wired and sewn together and as such the family was briefed by the mortician being advised against touching. My father burst into tears and ran from the building. I had never seen my father cry. I was shocked. The moment seemed frozen in time. This event would forever change my Dad. It occurred on my fourteenth birthday.

After the funeral life at home was more peaceful. Not as much yelling anymore. Dad was easier to get along with. The sadness would be there for awhile, but overall, even though this was a very traumatic event, life was somewhat easier.

That fall I went to high school. The Apalachin and Owego schools merged at this point. It was a different school building, some new kids as well as the old. But this change was different. It was better. These new classmates were cool as it were. We got along. The added bonus was they helped the other kids to lay off of me. I was feeling better and actually enjoyed school again. My grades were not great, but better and improving.

It was at this time I met Rachel. My life was about to change in ways I could not imagine.

2

My time in the hospital proved to be an education. However it would really be only the preparation for the real growth that would occur in later years.

I had been in counseling before my marriage ended. Both for anger management and for trying to save the marriage. I had studied psychology in college, but I learned a lot more hands on as it were.

Counseling was more of a question and answer session in which I did most of the talking. It seemed like a waste of time. I really was not ready to work as I would later come to realize.

I wanted the pain to go away immediately. I wanted to be able to sleep again. I wanted not to be a nervous wreck anymore. I wanted the pills to do it.

The doctor had told me that the pills were like eyeglasses. "They help you to see the problems in front of you, they do not make them go away, but allow you to see them so you can work on them."

I did not or would not get this. The pills were helping me stay calm and I was sleeping again finally. I wanted to go home but not to work.

What put me here in the hospital in the short term were too many major changes in my life. My wife had left me for another man, although it could have been me leaving for another woman as well. I had also just taken a major job transfer. On top of that the woman I was in love with decided after my wife left that she too did not want to pursue a romantic relationship with me. She only wanted friendship. Then my wife moved out of town with her guy and took my daughter with her. Because of all of this and the judge ordering a separation, we also had to sell the house.

All of these losses and also moving into an apartment complex were very heavy burdens.

I felt so guilty for all that had happened. My daughter was only four years old. She missed her Daddy and I missed her. I would come home from work after her mother moved out and cry for hours in her room. My own father had emotionally abandoned me, now I felt that I had abandoned my daughter.

It was terrible. I had really believed that I would get custody, but that did not happen. Once I realized that the only way to obtain custody was to prove the mother unfit, I tried to reconcile with my wife. Of course she had enough of me by then and would hear no more of it.

I was however a good father. My support payments were always on time and I visited as was written up in the separation agreement. I had been granted two days a week and every other weekend and every other holiday, but at two hours away it quickly became problematic for the two days a week visits. For both monetary reasons and for the emotional toll it took on my daughter, leaving her crying for her Daddy because of the short visits, every other weekend would have to suffice.

My marriage was at best an exercise in patience. I had developed a bad habit years ago called re-bounding. I had been engaged, or was planning to ask her. Eileen and I had been dating six months and were in love. I was nineteen as was she. Her mother who was in my opinion unhealthily close to Eileen obviously saw the possibility of me taking her away as very real. Friction developed between her mother and me and eventually came down to her telling Eileen that it was "him or me!"

See what I mean by unhealthy? A mother making her daughter choose between her boyfriend and her. Anyway, I decided to take the high road and not allow her to pursue that choice. I broke up with her and let her go. There was a story in the bible where a baby was being disputed by two women as to who the mother truly was. King Solomon known for his wisdom heard the two women's claims that it was their child. Neither would back down. The King declared that the child be cut in half, and present each half to each woman. The real mother spoke up asking the King to spare the child and let the other woman have him. The King of course realized the true mother was the one who would give her child up if it meant saving its life. He immediately presented the child to the real mother and ruled the other woman's claim as false.

I thought releasing Eileen would show her I really loved her and she would take a stand with her mother. Boy did I screw that up. Years later when I would see Eileen with her husband, her mother was always in the car with them.

I met Lucy shortly after that breakup. She had broken up with her fiancée because he had cheated on her. Misery loved company and we hit it off. We actually became good friends and that is where it should have stayed. I think it became a game of seeing if we could both make our ex partners jealous and get them back. It took on a life of its own however. Lucy started suggesting maybe we should date so we tried it on. Lucy had a huge ethnic family locally, I mean extended and all. I had immediate family here. One night after we were really drunk and petting heavily she asked if we should get married. I said "no, I am not ready for that." Lucy insisted and kept nagging me to propose. My error in patience was to do so to shut her up so I could go to sleep. She said yes and I went to sleep.

When I woke up the next morning the whole town was celebrating our engagement! I could not believe it. I clearly knew I did not want this, but my self esteem being what it was and the fact that Lucy was indeed an attractive woman I decided "what the hell, why not?." Big mistake.

I recall the day on the altar hoping Eileen would break in and stop the wedding. I also recall thinking that if I call it off now all these people that showed up would be so disappointed. I should have bailed, but that was who I was at the time. I remember somehow grieving Eileen the first two years of my marriage. I never was much of a crier prior to this. It somehow came intuitively and I only did it while alone.

Once I let her go in my heart I began looking at other women. There were three that I fell in love with over my seven year marriage. A neighbor that moved away before I could confess my feelings, a woman from church who I met at a bar after her divorce, and a friend from work.

The one from church and I had brief fling a few years after my daughter was born. She asked me to leave my wife but I could not bear to lose my daughter so we broke it off. By the time the third woman and I became close, I was ready to leave because I was not going to lose another opportunity to be "happy".

I had a few one nighters with other women before, during, and after these attractions. I had finally come to terms with my marriage. The kicker was that as close emotionally and in friendship that my work female friend and I were, she claimed not to return my feelings! Of course this was after my wife decides to leave!

My wife and I tried to have a house to save our marriage, a child to save our marriage, and God knows what else.

So here I was being stripped bare emotionally. I made a bad decision to take a job transfer which upon realizing was also a mistake, started my trip to the nuthouse!

As down as I was in the hospital, I also began to wonder if I was really that bad off. I saw people from all walks of life. The ones that scared me were the ones that had multiple personalities. I never knew what to make of them.

One woman who was a very attractive young Asian struck up a conversation after group therapy one morning. It was pleasant and I very much enjoyed her company. Of course the last thing I needed was a relationship. However, the conversation and company were great.

She sat across the room in the solarium where all of us took our meals. I was at a table with a few others at least fifteen feet away. All of a sudden she stood up and started yelling at some jerk, calling him all kinds of names and cursing at the top of her lungs. She made all kinds of accusations and threatened to kill him. I looked behind me to see who it was, but no one was there. I asked her, "Who are you talking to?" She said or rather screamed, "You, asshole!"

I quickly realized that she was the classic hospital patient in a mental ward! By this time the orderlies had come in and took her someplace to medicate her. It was an easy decision not to go near her anymore.

Then there was this woman who was being treated for depression. Her husband came to visit her every day religiously. He seemed like a great supportive guy. She meanwhile was getting day passes granted to her and going to a motel with another male patient and screwing all afternoon!

I decided to take my pills, do my occupational therapy making baskets, go to group and share what an idiot I was, talk to my shrink, and get the hell out of here as soon as possible!

At the time of my stay it typically took up to three weeks for the meds to reach their maintenance dosage. We were watched for side effects and how we responded, then sent home. I stayed out of work for an extended period as I attached a lot of anxiety to my job. Eventually I asked to be transferred back to my old position. When that occurred I went back to work.

During this time I had a relationship with another woman. It was for friendship from my point of view, but we were also attracted sexually. She began to fall in love with me, but I knew I did not feel that way. I knew I should leave but the sex was the best I ever had! I finally broke it off and did start my way through a lot of grieving. Even though I was not in love with her, it hurt to leave her.

After this I did remain single for five years. I dated sporadically and learned to keep my "gun in its holster." I worked, I dated, did all the day to day activities and of course went down every other weekend to get my daughter and bring her back to my apartment for the weekends. Taking her back Sunday evenings was tough. Coming home in the car alone and leaving her behind was tougher still.

More often than not I would cry in the car all the way home and maybe even more in the apartment. This went on for a good five years. I hated living alone; I hated not having my daughter. I felt guilty and blamed myself for all that had happened. They were dark years. A few times I was re-hospitalized for relapses and needed a medication change. I did not want to die, but I did not want to live either.

I wanted to stop hurting all the time, to stop feeling anxious. The meds only went so far. I went back to work each time not telling anyone why I was out other than a manager and hoping no one would find out.

I did not understand why I was afraid, or what might happen. I was a very confused young man. I did move out of the apartment complex and into a duplex with an elderly couple on the other side. I found this move to be peaceful.

It started to feel like I lived in a house again, which I missed terribly. This was helping me. It was a one bedroom again but more spacious. When my daughter came to visit she would sleep in my double bed with me. I was told this was not a good idea by my shrink. But I had no choice until now.

I bought a single bed to go against the wall across from the foot of my bed. I was told that having her in the same bed can somehow associate the daughter taking on the emotional responsibilities of a spouse. I did not comprehend this at the time, but I knew I should get her in her own bed. After a few weekends she adjusted to it.

I continued crying for almost five years off and on. Finally one day, after taking her home, I sat in my apartment and opened a beer. Something was different. I had let go. The acceptance was peaceful. I thought to myself, "This is okay living alone". "I am okay now." "I am okay with my daughter living elsewhere". "I am okay now". It was subtle, it was jubilant. The time in the desert was over. At least I thought so. The worst was over; however, the work was still ahead of me.

3

Rachel was a perfectly built beautiful young woman that looked more twenty years old than fourteen. I had never been attracted to redheads or blondes, usually always brunettes.

Cynthia had been a blonde though as was Kelly earlier. But Rachel was a babe. I liked her when I met her, but did not want to date her. She actually pursued me and after thinking about it over a weekend, I asked her to go with me the following Tuesday.

It did not take long to realize this was different than anything else I had ever experienced. It seemed we were falling in love. Yes fourteen is young, but this was clearly my first love and anything but puppy love. The tough thing was she was moving out of town and quite a ways away, like across country. It was only for six months, which seemed to me to be eternity at the time.

It hurt when she left, but we were still together. Our relationship comprised of letters being written and sent back and forth. This actually turned out to be a good thing. We really learned a lot about each other in detail in this way. The letters were always long on both ends. We were both good writers and expressed ourselves to each other well. Writing worked better than talking because the attention was held and did not drift as well as keep us focused on what was presented, rather than thinking of how to respond.

At the halfway point, around three months into the move, she called me! I had been alerted by one of her notes ahead of time as to the date and time. It was wonderful to hear her voice! After we hung up I was excited knowing I would see her in three months.

Spring arrived and I was outside enjoying myself and the warm weather when she called again. My mother teased me saying "You have a phone call and it's a girl!" When Rachel told me she was home and would see me in school tomorrow I became overjoyed!

We re-united and began a relationship that was to me storybook. The feelings and the acceptance were awesome. We dated, went places together, held hands in school and everywhere else, and walked with our arms around each other.

The guys that used to pick on me now respected me. I had a beautiful babe on my arm! But it was more than that. I really loved her. I never felt that way before. We were together almost two years. Two of the very best years of my life. She was my friend and my girl. I gave her a pre-engagement ring and told her I wanted to marry her when I was sixteen. She also wanted this; at least she said so at the time. Things were going well. My grades were up; I began playing bass guitar and found my way into a rock group.

Rachel would come to the practices and watch me play. I was on top of the world. I could get lost in her kisses, I was addicted to her. She started to play cymbals in a drum and bugle corps for women with a friend of hers. It started to take time away from me and I became jealous.

I had been asked to go to her practices as she had come to mine, but I kept putting it off as I hated losing my time with her because of them. Something inside me told me to go, but I resisted. When I finally thought it over and decided I would go, it was too late.

I was shocked when Rachel called me and asked to separate for the summer of my sixteenth year. I wanted to know what brought this on and why? She told me I had not been supportive of her in the drum and bugle corps. I acknowledged this and asked her for a second chance. She said no, we should see other people, and that it was only for the summer. I reluctantly agreed.

It was only six weeks as it turned out, but it was longer to me than the six months we were apart before. I was devastated. I kept myself in my room almost the whole time. This was probably my first episode of depression, but I did not realize it at the time. I just know that I ached inside.

She came back to me on my birthday. She had dated a couple of guys while I had no interest in dating anyone else. We were together again but it was not the same. I felt betrayed, abandoned, and very deeply hurt. We did not have the relationship skills or the support of our parents to work through this difficult time. Her mother had been divorced twice, and my parents should have been.

It became a matter of time as to the end of our relationship. It was said by people that knew us "It's a race to see who breaks up with whom first." I really did not want it to end. All I knew was it hurt real badly, and that I could not bear to have her leave me again. I had a tough time with rejection. I thought I could control the pain or even lessen it by being the one to take charge.

I broke up with Rachel only because I thought it was what she wanted. I wish we could have worked it out. I buried the pain inside of me and tried to get along with my life.

Shortly thereafter two things occurred. An offer from a better rock band came in which I jumped on, and I noticed one of my sister's friends checking me out. I asked her out and we started dating. Dating Diane took a lot of the edge off of the hurt I was feeling. It kept me occupied as did the band and going to school. It did get me through a dark time.

It was clear to me however that I did not feel for Diane the way I did for Rachel. I had no idea I was re-bounding at the time, only aware of the fact that it made life less painful. I had hoped Rachel would become jealous and come back to me. Of course she never did. We never spoke again, and I only ever again saw her once after when she was married and I was divorced from Lucy.

I spent eight months with Diane and broke her heart when I moved on. I had moved past the hurt and devastation of my break up with Rachel, or at least at the time I thought so.

The band went on for a year before it broke up, but we had some great times. We played several school dances and weddings. It was after that I began dating and using women. I drank heavily and turned to drugs. I found myself in trouble frequently. Somehow I made it to graduation and went on to college.

I never thought I would fall in love again until I met Eileen. The magic happened again. I knew a broken heart was repairable. I moved on with my life.

4

While my daughter was living with Lucy in Pennsylvania, I needed to get involved long distance with a few problems. My daughter was clearly having problems with her teeth coming in, and I was also concerned with her grades on her report card.

It was obvious to me that Lucy did not want to deal with either problem. She had stated that the teeth will grow in straight in time and that she herself had been a "C" student and turned out fine.

I began taking long lunches at work and making long distance calls from my area to Pennsylvania to get information from dentists and the school. I managed to have the school test her and I also was able to set up a Saturday morning consultation with a dentist in her area. The testing by the school supported an emotional and/or physical problem that was affecting her grades. It was recommended to have her tested by a neurologist to determine which it was, or if it was both.

The dentist did recommend an orthodontist. It was clear that some teeth needed to be pulled, and braces were needed. I set up appointments for an orthodontist and neurologist. The tests came back borderline between emotional and neurological. She was diagnosed with attention deficit disorder. Also it was suggested she see a child physcologist or psychiatrist for therapy and medication.

Lucy would hear none of any of this and refused to help pay. Fortunately she had re-married with the guy she left with so alimony was not an issue. I ended up footing the bill for everything and paying support as well as doing all the legwork.

I did get her started on the dental work and was able to set up weekend appointments with the child shrink back home when I had visitation. All of this was a mixed blessing. I was recovering from my illness by working with my shrink and focusing on the occupational therapy of caring for my daughter.

It was not long after my acceptance of living alone and not having my daughter that the news came that Lucy and family were moving back into town here. Once they re-located here, life began to get busier but easier. I transferred all her dental, school, and medical records up here and started working with local professionals.

I was also able to see her during the week as well as per the original custody agreement, prior to Lucy and I divorcing.

Also during this time I had been associating with a group of four women. We were all friends that did things together. Some of the women knew each other. I was able to relate to women easier than most men.

My two best male friends had moved away and my brother who I was close to was in the Coast Guard out of town. I needed deeper bonds than watching sports all the time and drinking beer! Two of these women I attempted to date. One felt safer as a friend but would later want me once I started dating the other!

Gabrielle and I met through a dating service. Once we met we decided to just be friends. We did go out on weekends frequently, while I did things off and on with the others during the week when I had time. Might be dinner, movies, or just walks, but it was good to do these things.

I was finally getting off the meds and was feeling better. Occasionally I would still have an anxiety attack, but they were further apart. During this time my doctor released me from his care. It felt good to feel alive again.

Gabrielle had an infant daughter that I enjoyed helping out with. I ended up being her Dad by association. Gabrielle and I took our daughters on a trip to the beach and amusement park that summer. It was during this trip that I began to realize that I was falling in love with her.

Gabrielle and I were complete opposites. I had never been in a relationship with this personality type. Some people thought we had our wires crossed so to speak. I was more female dominant in my personality while Gabrielle was more male dominant. Once I was sure of my feelings toward her, I told her. She seemed resistant for the longest time while we continued to do things together.

It took a while to win her over, but we finally started dating. My daughter became jealous of her at this point, even after telling for the longest time that Gabrielle and I should be boyfriend and girlfriend. I needed to take time with my daughter to make sure she was okay with things. She was cool after a while, but when I asked Gabrielle to marry me, her behavior reverted back.

Things were off and on with my daughter's behavior once the wedding was announced. But other things had been occurring with my daughter. Her mother was divorcing husband number two and was seeing other men. My daughter was going through another family breakup after finally getting used to her new one. She was now eleven years old and giving Lucy more than a handful. Lucy also had a second daughter by her second husband which Lucy was now requiring my daughter to baby-sit while she was out with her boyfriends.

It became increasingly difficult to keep Crystal on an even keel. But thankfully she was being treated by a very good local psychiatrist. I had no idea what lay ahead however.

Gabrielle and I found a house prior to our wedding. We could not pass it up so we made an offer and ended up buying it. We moved in together prior to marriage but we did keep separate bedrooms for the children's sake. We married the following fall and had the reception on our grounds. Both of our daughters loved the house and yard but mine did not like being apart from us. She had fears of my new family taking me away from her. I tried to re-assure her as best I could. It seemed to work.

Gabrielle and I were only married four months when just prior to Christmas I received a phone call from Lucy. "Do you want your daughter?!" she asked. I thought Lucy meant for Christmas visitation, so I said "I thought we had that worked out." She replied, "No, I mean do you want custody?"

I was shocked. "What do you mean? Why do you ask?" She replied, "I can not handle her anymore! Her behavior is horrible and she wants to live with you!" I explained to Lucy that if I did that, the support would cease, and that I would go through legal channels to make sure the "i's" were dotted and the 't"s were crossed. I asked to speak to my daughter and ask her about it.

She said that her mother was constantly babysitting other kids for money. She would leave my daughter in charge while she went over to see her boyfriend. She said she felt scared and just wanted to live with me.

I then spoke with Gabrielle about it. It was tough because we were just starting to get a sex life down after adjusting to sleeping together with her daughter in the other bedroom. This however was an opportunity to really help my daughter. I could not abandon her. Gabrielle agreed with some reservation, but we both knew this was the right thing to do. I told Lucy I would get her after the holidays. Lucy replied, "If you want her, get her now!"

December twenty-third at four o'clock in the snow I loaded up my sport coupe with all of my daughters belongings from her mothers. The car was packed but my daughter and I were finally re-united and heading home.

It was a wonderful Christmas gift! After the holidays I transferred her into her new school which she loved, and took care of all the legal things. It was only after about a week of everything being finalized that Lucy called and wanted her back. Of course I told her no and easily put down the contest.

My daughter was getting help in school and I could keep my pulse on things now. Her shrink released her to her medical doctor for providing medication and thought things would work themselves out now that she was in our care. Family life became what would seem normal now. Both my daughter and I were released from professional care.

The difficulties soon began after the first year. Dad now was in a traditional role. I had been the responsible father, but as far as a divorce goes, the fun parent to be with. Now the role reversed. I was the father that most children should have, and thus the disciplinarian.

My daughter did not adjust to this well. Gabrielle's daughter Hannah had grown up with me with no separation as such. She minded me easily, where my daughter, Crystal, had been gone seven years and missed these things with me. Crystal began to think that I loved Hannah and Gabrielle more than her. This is where the problems began. I assured her that was not the case and that I was just doing my job as a parent.

It seemed Lucy gave her her way. I did not. So we were off to the races after all! The battle for control was on. I had no idea how this was going to work out or where it was going.

Remember me saying I thought the pills would take care of me and that I thought I had done my work? I had not, as I was about to find out.

The path to awareness and personal growth had just been put in front of me.

5

I had received a referral for a child therapist and had called her to discuss treating Crystal. I had spoken to three people referred to me and had chosen Mary as the one I wanted to work with Crystal. I always choose three referrals or choices whether it be contractors for a job at the house or what have you. I pay attention to all three. I always trust my feelings and do not always go with the cheapest or most expensive. I trust my intuitive side and weigh all other considerations.

Mary was clearly the one I wanted. When Crystal and I went for our first visit, Mary interviewed us. This is where it became interesting. After speaking with us, Mary decided that Crystal should work with her counterpart across the aisle, Barbara. Mary decided to work with me. That's when it hit me like a ton of bricks! I clearly needed help! It had to work from both sides, the parent and the child! I knew I was in deep shit! However, I loved my child at least if not more than I love myself; therefore I knew it was time to find out exactly what made me tick! I was up for the challenge. I had no idea what was coming next.

As it turns out, the process was similar to working with psychiatrists, physcologists, and counselors. But with a twist! It was still having the therapist ask questions about real time issues, and me answering them. However then she would ask about my life with my parents and especially how things were in similar situations with them. She also kept probing at things I did not want to see or look at. She would find a way in her series of questions to get me to see things I did not want to see.

Family history was paramount to understanding how real time situations were being reacted to or dealt with. Very slowly I started to see how unconscious behavior was being passed on to my offspring.

In most cases I was re-acting my parent's behavior to my daughter and it was not always correct or appropriate. I very frequently projected onto my daughter and her me. Projection was something I came to understand what my father and I were constantly doing to one another.

Projection simply stated for those unaware, is we see a behavior in another that we see in ourselves. It can be good, bad, or indifferent. If good we may admire this behavior when another demonstrates it. We may criticize it when we do not like it, and remain indifferent if we have no opinion. For those of you fifty or above in age, projection is much like the old filmstrips we watched in school from a filmstrip projector. Imagine the film being our inner selves or ego; then imagine the projection of that film onto the wall. The picture on the wall from the projector represents the other person we see our behavior in.

My father and I frequently argued and projected onto each other. I came to an understanding about this. His most prominent projection to me was when he said to me, "You need therapy!" Understanding physcology as I took in college, I knew he meant at a subconscious level that HE needed it. However, since I emulated my father and was truly my father's son, I knew that this was most likely true for me as well. I was willing to go there where he was not.

I slowly began to see the pattern repeating with my daughter and I. We were also projecting back and forth. To stop this, I had to work on myself while she did her own work. From here on in this text I will describe what work I did and how it affected not only my relationship with my daughter, but how it affected relationships with all others!

Without going into each conversation with great detail, I will share with you many insights and experiences, as well as viewpoints as to my experience with what I learned and went through in my years with Mary. My daughter went through her own experience which only she can share. I can tell you this; things became much better after and during these years. I love my daughter and am eternally grateful things turned out well. This however is my story, Let's begin.

6

Emotional intelligence. Wrap your arms around that concept. Emotional intelligence is different than regular intellect. Simply put, it is clearing ones filter of any emotional baggage. As this process occurred, the pain and hurt falling away through my work with Mary, my intellect and perception became much sharper.

We have all heard of balancing heart and mind. This is exactly what occurred. It seemed I became much smarter, when actually it was that the pain was being removed. The illusions were removed. Behaviors and needs were removed. I was always this smart. My pain, illusions, and behaviors were clogging my processing filter. The freedom was worth all the work I had been through.

Now comes the word that no one wants to hear. Grieving. Yes, that is the key to all pain removal. I did not want to hear it either. But it is the only way to get through pain. Trust me, I know. I tried everything else. I tried eating it away and gained well over fifty pounds. That did not work. I tried gambling it away and lost a lot of money. That also did not work. I tried womanizing it away and tarnished my reputation. That did not work. I tried religion, yes religion. It is also a drug of choice for addictive behavior and pain. Religion has its strengths, I am not taking anything away from it, but to use it as an escape, it does not work either.

I tried drugs, alcohol, and even workahol! Being a workaholic did not help, it helped wreck one of my marriages, and did not change anything. Sex, drugs, alcohol, gambling, eating, church, working a career, all lead to repeating the behavior with no relief. Grieving did work. What had I to grieve? Plenty.

I was quick to learn how the process works with therapy. Again, it was working with a real time issue, and going back and learning how the past relates to the present.

Along the way realizations would come to my awareness with a past hurt. Instead of just talking about it, I would also be asked to FEEL it. "What did that feel like? What do you feel now?" At first I had a real issue with this. I always intellectualized my feelings, I did not feel them.

For example, Mary might ask, "What were you feeling when your father hit you?" My response would be something like, "It scared and freaked me out. Any kid would be. That's' just the way my Dad was back then. It was done to him, so he repeated the behavior." Mary would then ask me to work. "What were you feeling besides scared?" My response would be, "I don't know, I already told you."

She would pause, and then again come at it again. "You said you idolized your Dad and when he was not angry, you loved being with him." "Yes", I would reply. She would then lean in close and ask, "What did it feel like to have the hero you idolize hit you and hurt you like that?"

I began at that point to "get it." "I felt angry. It really pissed me off!" Mary would reply "that's okay. It's okay to feel angry." I knew it was okay to feel it. No one ever gave me permission to feel it though. That was her point and I received it well. She then asked, "What else did you feel?" I stayed with the anger as long as I could. I wanted to avoid where she was going, and she knew it. Finally we made progress as I surrendered to the process. "I felt betrayed and hurt." That's when the tears finally came and I began to sob.

"That must have felt awful?" Mary replied. I began to cry openly and as I did Mary's compassion in her demeanor and eyes made me feel comfortable doing so. I came to understand because I had never seen my parents cry while I was young; I had also chosen to hold these feelings inside. It was time for them to come out.

This is emotional work of which this is just one episode of this one particular issue. It took a few sessions on that one and I worked on it at home as well. I would cry until I was over that one issue. Sometimes listening to the radio, or watching television, or a real time incident would remind me of it and I would lose it and do my grief work.

I realized also that any good therapist worth their credentials would not waste their time or mine if I was not willing to do the work. They would dismiss me or not make another appointment.

Mary and I worked together for several years. I had much to process, but yes, it was well worth it. I would not trade the freedom I now enjoy to go back to the way I used to be for anything. No one likes going through the desert alone. It is dark and dry and can be frightening and very uncomfortable. But I had to go there to reach the destination I now very much enjoy.

I realized through this process as well that once some pain was removed, more awareness and very often more pain would follow. For example, after I had grieved being betrayed and beaten by my father, I came to understand I had also been emotionally abandoned by him. Abandonment is a huge issue to many. It sucks. It hurt as well. He was not there to teach me how to handle my emotions. I was not nurtured, loved, spent time with. Get over it some would say. Agreed, but the way to do that is to feel it, and grieve it. Getting over it is the natural by-product of the process.

I ended up grieving that and in the process became aware of the fact that I never had the dream relationship with my father that I so badly desired. I ended up grieving that as well. I would have loved to have played ball with him, gone fishing with him, or hunting or anything! Sounds simple? It was a valid loss, as Mary explained. I spent some time working on it.

My parent's marriage was not always peaceful. They fought fairly loud and aggressive at times. I had also became aware of the loss of a good happy relationship, both of my parents together, and them with me. It seems that I had a great deal of pain to grieve and I did not like it. I continued working through it however. I finally came to peace with it and was ready for more work.

Behaviors and illusions were coping mechanisms and by-products of those years. I had more to do.

7

It is said that as a child develops, the most formative years are birth through age five. Reason does not occur until age seven, or close to it.

So what do we do? It occurs to me thinking back to earliest memory and reasoning things out that at least in my case, I did the following. It is safe to say as children we are extremely observant. I observed very early on I was like my father physically. At least as far as the plumbing was concerned! For whatever reason I identified with him and wanted to be like him. However I also created myself with my mother as well.

I say created because at one point in therapy I arrived at the blame game. I blamed all my pain on my parents. I remained helpless and a victim until I realized what I am sharing with you now. Even though I had not reached the age of reason, I had already created who I was based on my observations of how my parents were. Children are also highly creative. I was responsible for who I was and how I behaved. That awareness is what finally set me free from being a victim and allowed me to work to become free.

I realized how unaware I had been before, and through this realized how unaware my parents were and still are to some degree. I also realized that even if I shared all this with them, or even with you the reader, no one other than myself will get it unless they or you go through their or your own process. I hope to encourage others that read this that are willing, to start on their journey to freedom.

I will not be able to reveal every nuance of my personality or my parents in this writing. However I wish to go over some of the major traits that needed to be understood and addressed in my life.

Perfectionism. I am a recovering perfectionist! This is the major player in my personality. I learned this from my Dad. Or properly said I created it by my observance of his behavior. This trait runs deep in my psyche, and tends to drive me nuts as well!

Everything has to be perfect!

It is a form of control. In my case a defense mechanism. In my mind if everything is perfect, I will not get yelled at or beaten. Ironically, I only choose those things that suit me to be perfect in! So I'd get into trouble anyway!

The most obvious traits of a perfectionist exercising control are subtle suggestion or sales. Intimidation, in your face aggression is possible in cases of abuse. Non-grieving showing no pain or emotion. Control at all costs.

These are the most readily observed traits in a perfectionist. Anger and temper when not getting the results desired are also among these.

The subtle condescending sales pitch. There is a certain tone used when trying to convince someone to do as you wish. Usually implied are worst case scenarios, and how to avoid them, and how doing whatever (the willed result of the controller) would be in your best interest. It was said of my Dad in latter years that he could talk you out of your socks and make you feel thankful you are barefoot!

If that strategy did not work, intimidation was a fallback method. That usually worked with an angry tone and being subtly threatened. The stern warning as it were. Of course that would eventually lead to the in your face loud threatening way if the results of the intimidation did not work.

Things never being good enough, even if they were. The perfectionist is always and forever looking to make it better. This behavior is the proverbial cat chasing its own tail. At least in my case, I was driving myself nuts!

I was also over punished as a child. Mom would discipline me, and then when Dad came home he would punish me again just to make sure I understood. He needed to be perfect. Later as an adult, I became hard on myself because of this. If no one else was there to punish me, I would punish myself.

This was the male side prominent behavior. I want to tell of my mother's side or the female side of the equation.

Living in the past or holding on. That is my mother's main behavior which of course I had also created in myself. Passive resistance, stubborn, non-grieving, living in the past, and resisting at all costs. My mother escaped by constantly talking about the past or dreaming about it. Sometimes you could tell as she zoned out or daydreamed of better times. She did not grieve these lost times and held on to her pain. She would dig in her heels to my father's demands and not argue or fight him, but definitely not do what he wanted if she was opposed to it.

So I also did all of that to a degree as well. Mixed with the other traits, I was really quite unique. Mom also had a hot temper. She never abused me or yelled at me, but she would get pretty mad sometimes. She would just yell at the world. I recall the time she threw a dish with dinner on it at my Dad. He ducked and it hit the wall sticking to it as it had mashed potatoes on it.

My mother also went into the hospital for depression at the same age I was when I had my episode. They brought her back with shock therapy, but she would never be the same woman I recall from my youngest years.

She is recovered from her depression as I had done, but she or my father have never done their emotional work that I share with you now that I have and continue to do.

These are the main players that operate within me. From these as coping mechanisms I also created illusions. The main ones are as follows; "Everything is good as long as I have control." "As long as I am perfect, I am not bad." "If I live in the past, I do not have to deal with my pain in the present. I have control there." "I must never feel or be helpless, or I am bad."

Understanding these illusions are at a very subtle unconscious level. I had no conscious awareness of these as a child, but always used and believed in them. My whole way of living and behavior in the world were based on the behaviors and illusions I have just described. I considered them normal, and for me at the time, they were.

Then there is the sub-illusion. I call it the marital argument (of my parents). This is, holding on to anger and trying to be perfect at the same time. I will come back to this one as I talk about learning to navigate illusions and behavior.

I also created a sub illusion of my own to cope. It is as follows; "Marriage will make me happy. Having a beautiful perfect wife or woman is what is needed." I need to explain this one. Some background first.

My father was abused as a child by his mother. Back then as told to me by my father, families were quite large. I do not recall the exact number but for the sake of illustration let's say there were twelve children in my grandmother's family.

I believe she was the oldest or old enough to have heard a conversation between the doctor and her father. The doctor explained that just after the last child had been born, death almost took the mother. The doctor told my grandmothers father, "No more children, Sir, this one almost killed her. The next one surely will." To which my grandmothers father replied, "One more please, doctor, just one more."

My grandmother was infuriated. She dearly loved her mother and now almost despised her father. Later when my grandmother met my grandfather and married, she became pregnant with my Dad.

It was a painful childbirth, to which also caused emotional pain. My grandmother desperately wanted a girl. It was not to be of course. She told my grandfather, "No more".

To this day I do not know if it meant no more children, or no more sex, or both. My Dad was of course an only child. He told me that his mother frequently dressed him as a girl. She had him in dresses and treated him abusively. My grandmother was also a perfectionist.

Dad later shared with me as I also surmised through therapy, that I reminded him of himself during those years of his torture. Those were the years I was beaten.

Coming back to the sub-illusion . . . As I said earlier, my parents were always busy both individually and as a couple. There was always a tension between them. However, there were those times when they were kissing, and or making out. There would be laughter, joy, and peace. It was not often, but it was obvious when it occurred.

My Mom had shared with me about how my Dad used to try to make her dress and act as his mother, which of course she refused and resisted to do. So it seemed in his perfectionism that he was both trying to control his mother and wife as one at the same time.

All I made out of this as a child was that it seemed to me at my young age, the way to being happy myself and perhaps to save my father, was find the perfect woman, settle down, and make out. This later of course became problematic! I had mentioned earlier that I always knew I wanted to get married from a very young age and that I did not know why but I did. I believe I have explained what I meant.

The real issues of abandonment, abuse, and my relationship with my father I never had, along with these traits and illusions all had been identified now, the trick was doing the work to grieve and navigate them.

8

Early in my relationships with women I became intoxicated while kissing them. At an unconscious level I was experiencing the sub-illusion I described in the previous chapter. Of course at the physical level I was also enjoying it. Similar to perfectionism, it never seemed to be enough. Again at the subconscious, it was not taking the pain away. It was not healing me or my father. But not knowing this consciously, I kept trying to do just that by craving more and more of the attention. I needed my "fix."

Being so needy led to self destruction in some key relationships with women I truly loved. I was so focused on my need that I ended up not giving the best part of myself as love to another.

It took me awhile to understand this. After being married the second time for a while, I observed that the people, times, and places were different, but it seemed the same as the last marriage and even similar to living at home with my parents.

Part of me realized this was coming to an awareness of understanding that in a mature relationship, both parties contributed and fed their relationship. We took on managing a home, raising children, nurturing each other.

Something was still missing. I found myself craving the kissing and making out and needing that fix. I understood I loved my wife and did not want anyone else. I understood that we had adequate making out periods and sex. I did not understand why I felt I needed more.

Some people go through up to six marriages, and I wonder if something like this is what fuels them, or if they just finally figure it out. I finally spoke to Mary about it. I recall her words after my discourse.

"Isn't time you grieved that and let it go?"

It hit me like a ton of bricks! I realized in that moment of conscious awareness that it was indeed an illusion, and that I did have to move on. I did not want to. This was something even being an illusion that had been with me all my life. It was what helped get me through. In the sense it was an illusion, it was like finding out Santa Claus was not real. In the sense of having to let it go, it was like losing a loved one.

As crazy as it may sound to some, this was a very deep loss. I loved this illusion! It hurt. But I treated it as a loss of a loved one and went through the grieving process. This one took a while. It was different grieving a belief system once I knew it was false, but a very real hurt. This belief no longer served me.

Prior to this realization, I had also found myself looking at other women again, even though I deeply loved my wife. I was thinking maybe another woman would help. After all that was also part of this illusion; needing a woman who is attractive to make out with, even though my wife was attractive. I realized that I can not have every woman I found attractive. But the urge to satisfy the illusion was there. I had to learn to navigate this, as Mary would later tell me.

All of the traits I mentioned in the previous chapter as well as this tendency needed to be navigated. Let me explain.

I will draw an illustration similar to the home computer. If I have certain programs on it that I need and a virus gets in, my computer of course is infected. If I can not rid the computer of the virus, I can contain it; keep it quarantined without destroying the other programs.

In the same sense, I can not change my traits and tendencies, but I can navigate them, live with them, while choosing not to be a victim of them. Understanding myself at a conscious level I can choose how to respond to my tendencies.

When I would see an attractive woman checking me out, the old system of needing her and making out with her feeling would of course kick in. Being conscious of this, I would work with the emotion, and navigate it. First above all, I would allow myself to "feel" it. I would use "self talk". I would say to myself, "yes I feel the need, but I understand that acting on this is only giving life to the illusion. It is only an illusion I no longer need as I have grieved it and let it go. I love my wife and need no other. I can not save my father only myself, and I do not need this to do so. I can not buy every car I like, nor can I have every woman I like."

During this brief self talk in my head and allowing myself to "feel" the need, not suppress it, the feeling would pass and I would be fine. The first time through this was cool once I experienced the result! Freedom from the need! I was on to something here.

As with any task I have learned, the more I practiced it, the better and faster I became at it. This particular navigation of this feeling became second nature, almost automatic where once a woman checks me out now, I just smile and move on. No thought required now.

The other traits I use similar methods. When I become caught up in trying to be perfect; again it is self talk after allowing the feeling; "I understand that I feel I need to be perfect. I also understand that my father can no longer hurt me. I can do my best without fear or worry. I no longer need be obsessed".

It works with any of the traits for me. "I do not have to live in the past, I can let go of it and move on. This was Mom's way that I no longer wish to employ".

The key with any one of these navigation skills is to FEEL the particular feeling, illusion, or tendency. My mistake for years was trying to suppress them. We can not suppress who we are. If I have a habit I do not like, it is still part of who I am. To suppress those parts of myself I only deny them.

Ever try to ignore a child? They will keep after you until you give them attention. Same with tendencies. Whenever I denied that I was angry about anything, what would eventually happen would be after a number of things making me angry and not acknowledging them, I would explode and throw one hell of a tantrum!

I learned to express the feeling rather than to suppress it. A feeling or tendency can be like a demon, or in fact a demon may simply be a suppressed feeling or tendency. It will chase me to hell and back until it is acknowledged. After all I created it. I can not deny my own creation any more than I can deny myself.

Any more when something makes me angry, I simply say to myself aloud or in my head, "I am angry about this". That sometimes is all that is needed.

Grieving past hurts, grieving illusions that no longer serve, and learning to "feel'. These are what I needed to heal. The freedom on the other side is well worth the effort.

After having gone through most of my work, I began to think about things like Alzheimer's disease and also alcoholism. I wonder if Alzheimer's could simply be a mind loaded with undone emotional work and unawareness? I wonder if the alcoholic needs the drink to bury the pain? Would he no longer need the drink if he or she did the deep emotional work? I do not have the answers but it does beg the question.

My biggest block in getting to the point of doing the work was allowing myself to feel helpless. Having observed so much controlling behavior by my parents and creating it in myself, this was a tough one for me. But when I did allow myself to feel helpless, I found I did the work more easily. The awareness came more easily.

I do not know if I would have ever put myself through any of this if it were not for my daughter. Putting her first and "sacrificing" myself as it were brought me to this freedom. I became the hero to myself that my father never was.

Mary did not teach me to navigate; she simply helped me identify the issues. She allowed me, in fact insisted on me doing the work. Once I identified an issue, I would ask her; "What do you want me to do?" I would press on; "Tell me what I should do?" Her reply would be, "I can not do that. It is up to you."

In the grand scheme of things it was only right. I created who I was, and I had the power and the choice to recreate myself. People do not really change all that much, but they can and often do grow.

Growth, even emotional growth is painful. Remember growing pains in our arms or legs when we were children? Emotional growth is no different. I mentioned earlier about Mary confronting me on the illusion, and my recalling it hit me "like a ton of bricks?" Awareness hitting me, emotional intelligence revealing itself. This is what I call a "light bulb moment". Finally getting it. These moments of awareness or emotional growth were my measuring sticks along the way.

Most of my life I hated cats. Kittens, cats, were always victims of my abuse. I did some nasty things to them that I will not mention here. I never took ones life though. I never understood why I did not like them. I just accepted it.

During my analysis, and making discoveries along the way, I finally understood why. Again, another "light bulb" moment.

I was told by relatives and by looking at my baby photos, that I was a cute, cuddly little boy. Many of these traits a kitten or cat has. Because of the beating I took at the hands of my father as a cute, cuddly, little boy, I learned or created a part of me that despised that part of myself. I projected this image onto a kitten and or a cat. I often treated them as my father treated me.

Once I became aware of this, and began to understand why my father did what he did, I began to grieve and heal and understand that there was nothing wrong or bad about that cute little boy. Once I knew this emotionally, not just intellectually, I began to love the little boy in myself. I now love cats and especially kittens.

Gloria was my wife's cat when we met. She was part of the package deal I accepted when I asked my wife to marry me. Gloria and I had some rough times early on. But suffice to say during my therapy and coming to this awareness, we eventually became buddies. I grieved long and loud when she died. I vowed to her as she died in my arms I would honor her and all cats from now on.

We bought Nola as a kitten and at the time of this writing she is a deeply loved cherished healthy pet. Actually she is family. Having her since she was four months old, I was able to train her, as much as one can a cat, and she does mind me. It is freeing to be able to love and adore this cute creation of God.

9

Another creation of mine in my personality that I observed in my mother besides living in the past is holding on to it, or even just holding on in general. I recognized this in my current wife as a projection.

My first wife had many of the traits and behaviors of my father. This time around was more like my mother.

Gabrielle's mother I learned had passed away when Gabrielle was only eighteen. She did not mention her mother much, but she really doted on her daughter, who, I raised from the time she was in diapers. Even though she is not blood, I love her same as if she was.

Any time I would ask curiously about her mother, Gabrielle was very elusive. She was open about her relationships with her Dad or even ex-boyfriends. It did not take long for me to realize that she was carrying this pain around with her. She was not living in the past, but boy was she holding onto it. She had never grieved her mother.

I took it upon myself to help her with this. At this time I had not yet been in therapy with Mary. I had not been married, we were dating. It really was not my place to do this, but I saw it needed to be done, so I did.

I would ask questions and push the envelope until she started crying. She thought I was being cruel and often would say, "Stop picking on me!" I would reply, "I am not picking on you, this needs to come out."

I stayed with it for the first two years we were dating. She slowly did finally grieve the mother she lost fifteen years ago. I recall the first and second time we went back to her hometown to visit her relatives, including her Dad and step-mother. I met several aunts and uncles and her sister and nephew.

During these visits she would go by herself to her mother's grave and come back very somber and distant. She would slowly come back to being herself after these visits.

I learned from her that her Dad and mother had known the current step mother and her late husband through church. The stepmother's husband had passed away very close to the same time as Gabrielle's Mom. Her Dad and stepmother were married within a year of each losing their spouse. I mention this because at the time of this writing, my father in law has been gone a few years now. As was pre-arranged when they married, they were to be buried with their former spouses. One comment out of my step mother in laws mouth according to my sister in law was, "He left me so he could be with her." She referenced Gabrielle's Mom in that statement. This clearly showed me that he had never grieved his first wife and that the second was very much aware of this. I could see why my wife was like she was in the non-grieving respect.

The spring after the second time back to see her relatives, Gabrielle went back again, this time without me. Later that year when her sister came out to visit, she shared with me that Gabrielle had asked her to go with her to the mother's grave. This was important for two reasons. The first being she never allowed anyone to go with her. The second was what my sister in law told me. "Jeff, she cried like a baby, like it just happened." I told her how I had been working on her to try to help. I was told that she had not shown much emotion at the funeral. Clearly my efforts were bearing fruit.

The following year we went back again to visit my wife's relatives. Gabrielle asked to use my car to go to the cemetery. I asked should I go with her, but she said no. I offered no protest and let her go. She came back later in a noticeable good mood and smiling. I knew then we had accomplished what we were supposed to. She had let go and was at peace.

She since that time has been able to speak of her mother without the pain and quite fluently I might add. We finally married that fall or rather late summer.

When my father in law passed a few years ago, since he was to be buried with his first wife, I finally accompanied my wife to visit her mother's grave. With all we had been through, it was an honor to finally attend.

Why do we need to hold on so? Any time I see an old television episode of a favorite show, or read an old book again, it means something different than it did the time before. A Bible reading has taken on different meanings at different times in my life. We are constantly growing; we can not go back to what we are holding onto. Even if we could go back in time, it would not be the same. We have grown and are not who we used to be. The perspective would be different, we may make different choices, and it would feel different.

Even if we could go back exactly the way it was, we would only repeat the same choices not armed with the new awareness.

So what is the point? It is only because we are not at a conscious level of understanding that we hold onto things. Speaking of that, I had mentioned earlier in this chapter that noticing holding on was a projection.

I myself would later discover a deep hurt that I had never dealt with and was unaware of. It would soon be my turn to grieve the past. But when this awareness revealed itself to me, I was already practicing and working with Mary. It did catch me by surprise, but I knew what I had to do.

10

I had been married at the time five years and had re-acquired custody of my daughter and was now working with Mary.

I remember sitting out on the deck enjoying a warm summer day, drinking a cold one when I heard laughter next door. My neighbors also had an in-ground pool with an adjoining deck. Out in the pool was the youngest teen with his new girlfriend of about the same age. I recall watching for a while as they splashed and affectionately grabbed and tickled each other. They were obviously enjoying first love and each other. It reminded me of my first time in love and it made me feel good to watch them.

They say first love never dies. I can understand that in a few ways. Usually, not always, ones first encounter is during the teen years. We are still at home and do not have to consider a career, a home, bills, and children among other things. It is easy to get caught up in the grandiose illusion and get lost. It has been said that when one falls in love, it is actually a projection of the best of ourselves. So in theory we fall in love with ourselves!

Sometimes people wonder about what it would be like to go back with their first love. I would say to them that putting it in perspective, based on the paragraph above, it would not be all that different from the relationship they are in now. Different parties and problems, but relationship issues nonetheless. There would still be things that needed working out.

But also not to take anything away from first love, we do always remember them and based on what one of my favorite authors, Neale

Donald Walsch writes in the Conversations with God series, "A man never stops loving a woman he has loved." "Even after several relationships," I believe he added. Those times are special.

Getting back on point; watching those two stuck with me long after they left and my day went on. I could not put my finger on it. I had passing thoughts of Rachel, my first love. I wrote it off as just an association of relevance to the event I had witnessed.

During this period of time, my step-daughters father had been dating a red-haired woman, and I would see her occasionally when he dropped off Hannah as she was with them. Rachel was also red-haired and she again entered my thoughts. I also associated this with the event of relevance at the time.

Rachel began creeping into my thoughts more and more. I had not thought of her in years. Why was she so prevalent now?

I had recently had my first experience with a massage therapist. She was a former work colleague. She had left her job to go to school to learn this and was very good. The first time for me was like taking a drug or getting laid for the first time. I felt so good it took a few minutes in the car to gain enough perspective to drive!

During this time my brother was dating and living with a young divorcee that was also learning massage therapy. She was young, vibrant, and beautiful; with red hair! When she graduated she offered me a massage and based on my previous experience, I was eager to have one. My wife is a blonde but does have a strawberry shade to her hair at times, and has freckles like Rachel, but not as pronounced. My wife is not much of a toucher or hugger. Rachel was very "touchy feely" as some say.

My brothers girlfriend, the massage therapist also had freckles and was very much "touchy feely" and a massage therapist as well. When she started on me with the massage, it was as if memories of Rachel came flooding out. As relaxed as I was physically during and after the massage, my sensory input of Rachel was now overwhelming me.

Neale Donald Walsch in one of the books in the Conversations with God series also writes that memories exist not only in the brain, but in the skin itself. I can vouch for that based on this experience.

I quickly realized with help from therapy that I had never grieved losing Rachel. I had only buried her deep in my subconscious. When fully realized, it was like it just happened in that moment. It hurt deeply and even though over twenty five years had passed, it was fresh.

There was a period in time when I hated Rachel and did not give a damn about her. I realized now that was an attitude of control to keep the pain away. As I openly wept for the loss of a woman from the distant past, I realized I could never ever hate her.

This became one of the toughest losses of my life. I felt at the time I could not share it with anyone, especially my wife. It seemed so weird, but then again no. I recalled helping Gabrielle deal with her mother's death, so I used the same technique with myself and my therapist.

One thing I deeply regretted was never keeping in contact with Rachel. Any other women I had been in relationship with, I had at least an opportunity after the fact to talk to them about our relationships and heal from them. Not to mention I was friends with some of them and acquaintances with all of them.

Not with Rachel did I have any of this. We never spoke again after we ended it. I ran into her once after her first child was born and said hello. She barely acknowledged me with a far away look and said she knew who I was by my eyes. That was it. Someone who meant the world to me and I never spoke to her again. This hurt more than any of the other relationship losses. It also took a very long time and lots of hard work to move through it. To this day at the time of this writing we have not spoken.

I thought I saw her one day at the mall but was not sure if it was her. Although I have since moved through my grief and shared all of this with my wife, I still feel I have unfinished business with Rachel.

What business? I am clear that I am happy with my wife and my life right now. However, Rachel was someone who deeply influenced my life. If given the chance I would like to say several things to her.

"I never wanted to break up with you. I wanted to work things out but did not know how. I could not bear to have you leave me again. I thought I could control the pain if I left you, rather than waiting for you to leave. I was wrong. I am sorry for not having kept at least a friendship going. There were so many times I wanted to call you, even years after we split. I always seemed to talk myself out of it."

"I'm sorry I was not the man I needed to be for you, for me, for us. You were one of, if not one of the most influential people that came into my life. You meant the world to me. Even though I have moved on and am happy now, I will always hold our time together in my heart. Thanks for being in my life."

I think I could let go completely at that point. Something inside says I need to say that to her to finish it. Or maybe open a friendship. At the time as I write this I feel that I would be invading her life to call her or write her. It seems a spontaneous meeting would be the only means open to me. I hope it can happen, but if not I wanted to include it here in this work.

Perhaps putting it down on paper will be the final point of letting go.

Grieving this loss was also done in stages. I grieved the original hurt, then the loss of friendship, or the possibility thereof, and finally what might have been. I find not being able to talk to her again the most frustrating.

However many of us including my wife do not get that chance. Gabrielle had to grieve her mother long after she was gone. Putting pen to paper, talking with a trusted confidante, or even talking to the person imagined helps get out the pain. For who know? Spirit may be able to transcend time and space and be present when we beckon, even though we do not see them. I like to believe in possibilities.

At the time of this writing I decided to include the words of the letter that I wrote to Rachel. I of course never sent it for the reasons mentioned earlier. I had written it during the deepest part of my grieving with sobbing and tears to help me process my hurt. At the time I wrote it, I felt I needed to have that conversation with her. But having moved through my grief, at this time, rather than a need, it is simply a preference. I would still enjoy talking to her and sharing it. This time now, it would no longer be for me, but for her, if needed, and if not, just to affirm what is so.

An emotion can either be fulfilled or grieved to be free of it.

11

Once identified a behavior or tendency any of which I have listed or others, can be navigated. My way is just that, my way. I am no expert, and I do not pretend to be. Grieving I have found is the only way to heal from pain. Once the hurt real or perceived is there, it has been created and to be free of it, grieving is the tool to use.

To this day I continue to come to different levels of awareness. Old hurts occasionally come up, and I simply allow the feelings to come and I cry and very quickly move through them. Now that I have moved through all the past deep hurts, I am quicker to move through new ones.

The key to navigating for me again is allowing myself to both feel helpless, and to feel the emotion at the time. Trying to navigate or recreate a tendency while not allowing the feeling only leads to failure, frustration, and giving up.

I still have not mastered my temper fully, but do have a greater success ratio than ever before. I succeed most of the time. The times I am not consciously aware of it, it does get the better of me. Once down that road, I can only ride it out until it passes.

But overall I am a free man. Depression and anxiety can be overcome. I have survived it with no relapses. I am so much more healthy now as well. I hope this writing will help those struggling with these afflictions. I also put this to anyone who is not going through these diseases who simply wish to grow and discover more of themselves. This is my on-going challenge to myself. Continued self awareness and improvement.

It seems to me that if we as a species should wish to advance, it would be the goal of every individual on the planet to challenge themselves in this way. I would love to see us move away from competition to cooperation. It of course would require giving up and grieving things that no longer serve us. This in some cases would take us back to grieving and letting go.

Sometimes I feel overwhelmed and cry for no reason. During these times I used to try to figure out what was going on. Anymore I just let the tears flow figuring that whatever it is, it needs to come out. I do not wish to carry any of that pain around anymore. I do not necessarily need to know what event triggered it.

Things from the past also "pop-up" from time to time. I recall listening to satellite radio one evening when a song came on that I remember hearing on my transistor radio in my back yard in Endwell. I never favored the song itself, but in recalling the memory of that warm summer day in my beloved back yard, I realized I had never grieved leaving Endwell for Apalachin. I allowed the tears to come, had a good cry and was good to go after twenty minutes. This issue never came up again, and in simply acknowledging and moving through it, I healed and was freed from it. I could list many examples of this, but I hope that one suffices.

I recall longing for the perfect woman of my dreams to show up and make me happy. That longing continued to go on into my first marriage and kept on until I married my current wife. I realized in my first marriage that I had married the wrong one. The longing however I came to understand was a combination of my illusion to help me cope, and of not having grieved my past.

I now am finally free of this longing having done my emotional work. I have also been able to help my children work through any issues I see repeating themselves.

As I allowed myself to feel helpless, I was able to manage Crystal much easier. Rather than give her the power to control me or my wife and step-daughter, I would allow her the behavior I did not wish, and stop fighting it. However, I always imposed consequences. I also gave her an opportunity to earn back any privileges I took away. For example, if she was grounded for two weeks she could earn back a week by doing various assigned chores to my satisfaction.

I learned to stop reacting when she did the things that angered us. I stopped reacting and remained calm when she threw a tantrum after I grounded her.

By giving up control other than that of myself, she quickly learned she could no longer control me. I only can control myself and no other. This also set a positive example for her as we both continued working in therapy.

When Crystal finally grew up and moved out, I did grieve the life change. It was different this time though. This was how it was supposed to be. The child leaving the house as an adult. When she was taken from me at age four through the divorce, I cried my heart out. I let her go all those years ago. This time, even though there were tears, it felt right. I had a good twenty minute session and was good to go.

This is different for my wife. As my youngest left for college, my wife loses it for a long time, every time, after every visit home. I understand though that it is the first time, as it were, for her to let her child go. I understand that this is under "normal" circumstances. It is a loss for a parent to let the child go. I guess I had it earlier than a lot of people. It is okay to grieve both for the parent and the child as this is a time of transition for each. It seems to me to be quite human.

Crystal married a few years after leaving. When I gave her away at the altar, and when I danced with her to the father and bride dance, there were no tears for me. Having already grieved and let go, these were very happy moments for me, and I treasured them.

I really enjoyed that wedding. I have gained a son in law I do cherish as my own son.

I find it so freeing to be able to write about it.

12

In my experience I have found that repressed or held back emotions do much damage. These are some of my observations as well as Neale Donald Walsch's;

Repressed pain or hurt becomes depression if unexpressed.

Repressed fear becomes anxiety if unexpressed.

Repressed love becomes possessiveness if unexpressed.

Repressed envy becomes jealousy if unexpressed.

Repressed anger becomes rage if unexpressed.

I have found it challenging in some circumstances to learn how to express these feelings constructively. Feeling and navigating has been what continues to work for me.

I am still discovering new ways to work with some of these feelings. Being conscious is the key. I must be aware of what is going on consciously to navigate and feel. I mentioned earlier I was having some success with anger management. I had a "light bulb" moment of awareness come to me the other day after I became angry and started down the road to speaking excessive colorful metaphors.

I discovered that the perfectionism is where it usually starts at the sub-conscious level. The problem I find in being a perfectionist or recovering one is that I demand the best from myself, and everyone else. This includes nature, sports teams, and cars, whatever. It is one thing to expect it from myself, but from anyone or anything else is of course insane.

If I were aware of that before I became angry, I of course would be navigating it. It has been sneaking up on me for the longest time. I did not know that was causing me to become angry.

The second part of the tantrum was again the marital argument. I am not only expecting perfection from whatever I am angry at or whomever; I am also holding onto it and trying to control it as this occurs. Since I have already allowed the perfectionism to subtly control me, now the other tendency starts to fight it. Passive resistance. Only moments now before the tirade begins.

On top of that I have been taking it very personally when something disappoints me. Three tendencies from the past operating together. My trick now is to be aware of the first. It starts there. Then I can navigate it, without having to lose my temper.

Once I have lost my temper, I can only ride it out. I can self talk and do the work with the perfectionism first, allowing myself to feel, and then work the other two traits. I am hopeful and excited that I may finally master this last major piece of my personality.

Having brothers and sisters that are now also in therapy, I still find other things about myself to work on. It is wonderful having perspective. They know me well, and are working on similar issues and many of the same ones, and are quick to point them out. I do find it helpful.

Another thing I wanted to bring up was what a worrier I used to be. I was constantly worrying about everything! This of course had a lot to do with the control issues. After identifying the previously mentioned control issues, I slowly stopped worrying about anything.

Worry to me, I discovered is nothing more than negative energy. It is perfectionism run amok! I can in any instance choose to either react to a situation, or navigate it as it comes at me. Worrying about it happening is wasted time, emotion, and energy. I can take steps to prevent various things from happening, but in the end can not control them. I can only control myself.

I have found much freedom in not worrying. I also find with all the freedom I now enjoy, that things occur to me naturally. I do not have to think as much. I just notice when something or someone needs attention and simply move into it. I take whatever action is needed in those situations. Life is much simpler.

It seems to me that this will be ongoing for me for the rest of my life. It is normal at this point. Like a pilot flying a plane from one destination to the next. Things change from the time of take off. Storms brew, winds change, traffic may increase, and the like. The pilot is constantly adjusting his flight plan and navigating whatever conditions exist until finally reaching his destination. It is natural to me now.

I had no clue how far behind normal people if there are any I was. With most all of the past behind me now, and the future yet to come, I strive to live in the present moment. It has been a challenge as I find my mind constantly drifts unless I am concentrating on what I am doing. I mean, riding in the car for instance, rather than taking in the moment fully, I am thinking this or that, or listening to the radio, or daydreaming. Yes, it is human. I do wish to be more alert and "take time to smell the roses." I am working on it.

13

Earlier in this writing I had mentioned never having seen my parents cry as a child. I had mentioned it would be detrimental in later years. It was of course. The events I described that I had buried and not grieved were major players leading up to my depression. I continue to stress what goes on in the formative years of childhood. I created the non grieving child and did so at my own expense. Thankfully I learned through therapy how to go back and identify events and creations that were holding me back in the present.

The anxiety was actually worse than the depression. Both were painful together, but I found nothing more painful than anxiety attacks. Once I understood them, I learned to navigate them. They finally stopped. I have not had one in over twenty years now.

Anxiety is repressed fear. Mine was at a subconscious level. It started with being afraid of my father. I was terrified of both being beat up and rejected. This fear eventually projected out onto any authority figure. It also projected out onto the punishing God I grew up with.

With all of what was going on at the time, when these attacks were occurring at work, I was afraid of being fired because I was missing time and could not figure out what was going on in my own head. This was right before my hospitalization. I was afraid of not being able to care for my daughter. I was afraid God would punish me. I was afraid I would never get better. I also kept all this inside. Hence the panic attacks.

Guilt is not a normal emotion. It is taught. It is used for control. Adding guilt on top of fear increased the intensity of the anxiety attacks. I had no awareness of any of this at the time.

As I learned to express fear, I also created a navigation tool for myself to deal with it. I began again with feeling the fear, then self talk, again silently in my mind. "The father of my past can no longer hurt me. I no longer need be afraid of him. My boss and my God are not projections of my father. They are not out to get me. They are looking out for me. I need not be scared anymore. Guilt is not natural, I need not feel guilty, but rather take any responsibility for myself that is required." The attack would disperse and my mind would become clear. I would feel at peace.

Rather than try to rationalize the fear away I would feel it then navigate it. Worked just as quickly as the tranquilizers! I no longer do guilt at all. If something should trigger any fear now I face it head on. I have found the only way to conquer fear is to go right at it and confront it. I will no longer allow fear to control me. In fact, my anger is a tool I now use to push myself at any fear and subdue it!

I also use the perfectionism as a tool. It serves me well in finances. It causes horrible issues with relationships!

Depression and anxiety are beatable if one chooses to confront them and is willing to do the work.

14

In closing I wanted to say there is a fine line between perfectionism and the pursuit of excellence. The line defines obsessive behavior and doing ones very best. I could continue with many other tendencies and illusions, but then I would be trying to be controlling by being perfect!

I hope having opened up my soul and intimate times in my life will help others. That is the purpose I had in mind when I started this text. If it has not been helpful in that way, dear reader, I hope it has at least been entertaining.

I would like to thank all those that have inspired me to share my time with you. Everyone mentioned and even those not mentioned here, including my family and friends and all outside influence.

Neale Donald Walsch who deeply inspired me with his writings, especially the Conversations with God books. Elton John whose music has always brought through the feelings and emotions I experience, and help me process them.

The New York Mets who have allowed me to deal with much frustration and also great joy.

My Creator whom I now understand is a loving deity, not a punishing one.

My family and especially my wife and daughters who give me focus when I really needed it.

The gift of music, my true first love. Music has helped me feel, feel my grief, feel my joy, and feel period. To all of you, the readers to whom this hopefully brings insight or useful information to use or share with another.

To my counselors, therapists, and doctors, whom without, I would not be here.

To all things seen and unseen, to all those loving spirits, thank you. Peace, love, and joy to all. Au Revoir!

15

As I end this text, I wish to inform you, that it has taken three years to finish. I have taken frequent breaks in writing. Most of the bulk of this was hand written in a journal during the winter months as inspiration occurred. Once good weather arrived, I put my work aside to go out and get busy with it.

Before I close, I did wish to share something that occurred relevant to the preceding chapters.

I randomly walked into Rachel in the Wal-Mart parking lot! She remembered me and we embraced. We began e-mailing each other after that. I finally was able to tell her all that is in one of the previous chapters, and we are now friends.

However, something surprised me. She does not remember much of our relationship! She recalls we went out but not much after that. I needed to fill her in, but still nothing.

I am glad that I was able to apologize to her and tell her how important she was to me. I find though that it stings that she can not remember.

I can only come up with two reasons for this in my mind. First, is that my breaking up with her did indeed hurt her to the point that she suppressed the memory of the relationship. Second, she never felt the same way about me, and that I made it out to be bigger than it was based on my illusions and who I was at the time.

I may never know which it is, as I can not control her, only myself. It does leave me feeling a loss inside. I can only do this; grieve it as a loss. Treat it as the illusion it seems it was and let go of it. I am doing this and know I will be fine and be free.

Should she recall it as real, it will be a treasure lost that is found. In any case I will have no expectation or attachment to the past, and can be the best friend I can be to her.

Christmas is approaching as I end this. The rest of the winter will be getting it typed! Thanks for joining me on the ride. I wish you all the best!

www.ingramcontent.com/pod-product-compliance
Lightning Source LLC
Chambersburg PA
CBHW020408290526
45785CB00005B/2474